NOT JUST BYE !

Make it good! Stories for Life

Book Author: **Stories for Life**
Title: **Not just bye!**
© 2015 Printing for Life

ISBN-13: 978-09940339-0-1

NOT JUST BYE !

Make it good! Stories for Life

**What does it mean
to say goodbye
to someone
who makes you feel happy?**

It means that
sometime before
there was probably a 'hello'
with a warm hug and a big smile.

Imagine it is almost Christmas and your favourite
uncles and aunties have just arrived from their long trip
(half-way across the world)
to celebrate with you in your very own home.

Christmas holidays are your favourite
time of the year for many reasons:

So many people to play with
and spend time with, so many presents
and exciting activities.

Much sooner than you would like

———————————————————

the expected happens:

Christmas is over.

But thankfully something else happens every year
after Christmas.

A few days
after Christmas,
on the last day of
the year ....

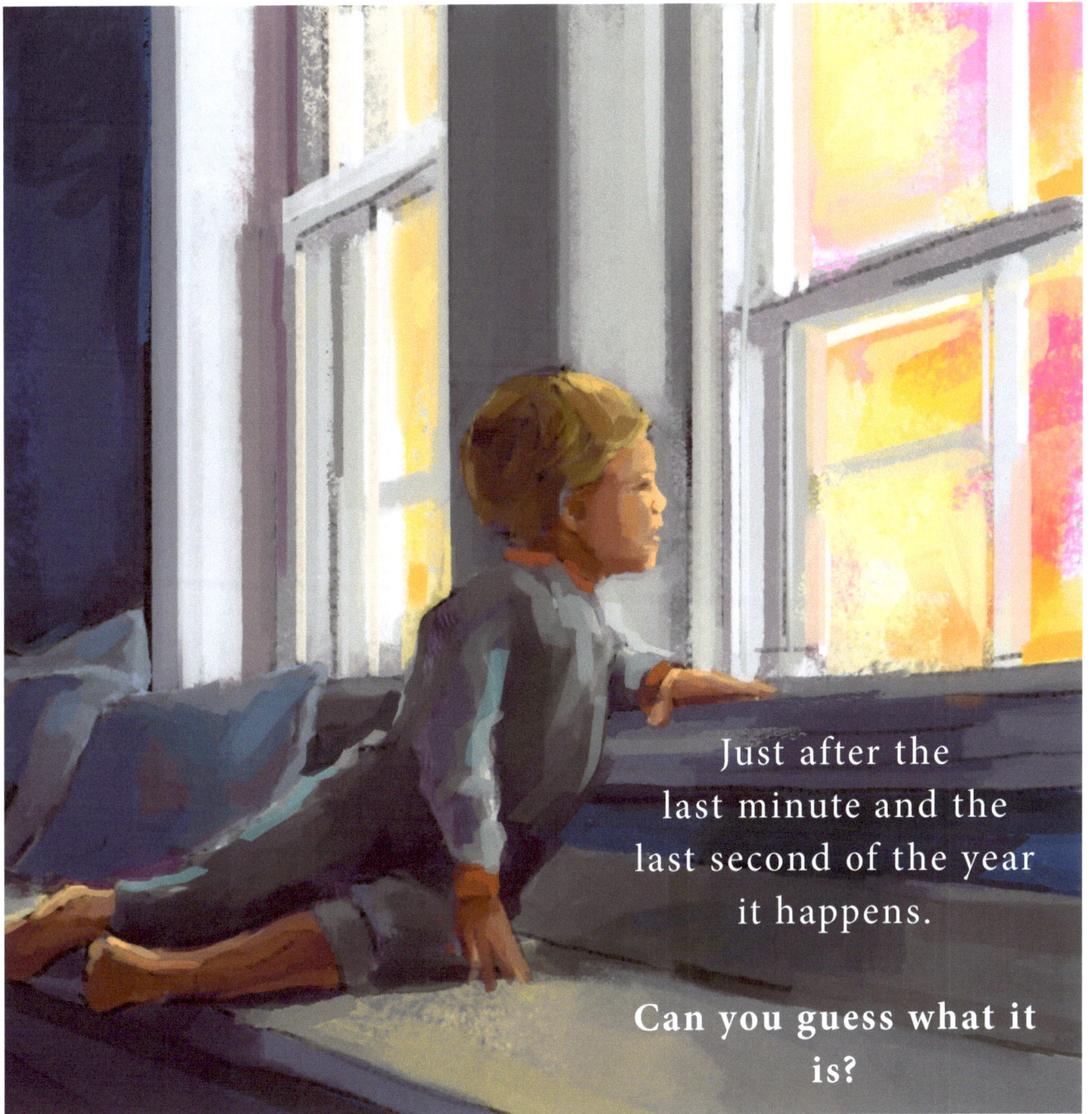

Just after the
last minute and the
last second of the year
it happens.

Can you guess what it
is?

Wooooooosh BANG!

A sky full of wonders:

fireworks bringing in the new year.

HAPPY NEW YEAR

Beautiful colours lighting up the night sky.

Fun shapes and forms.

Can you see, hear and smell it?

Soon after you hear the sounds of cheers and laughter,
well-wishes and toasting.
Not the type of toasting
you do with bread and a toaster.

This type of toasting involves raising
your glass and drinking together to wish someone well or
celebrate something
special. We'll come back to this
but first let's continue your story.

After toasting there is much cheering
and celebration!

Soon it is time to switch off
the light and to everyone
say goodnight.

Saying goodnight is like
saying goodbye
to the day and hello to
the night.

You fall asleep. Can you hear yourself snore?

Wait a moment, something's happening.

Something is tickling your nose...

What's happening?

Where's that coming from?

The sun is beaming through the window

and tickling your nose....

Hatschu! Hatschu!

A loud sneeze!

Sorry two loud sneezes!

One after the other echoing through the room ...

All the way throughout the house...

Resulting in everybody waking up!

A new day! The first
day of
the New Year:

New Year's Day!

In our story this is the day to say goodbye to your favourite aunties and uncles because they have to travel back home half-way across the world.
That's a long way.
Saying bye isn't easy and doesn't feel nice, when you have had such a good time.

But isn't it a little bit like saying goodnight?

How can you make saying bye good (a true ˋgoodʹ-bye)?

Does it become good through:
Head-butting your uncle?
Screaming at your aunty?
Kicking the door?
Running away?

Of course not! You're right.
But how do you make it so it's a real goodbye?
Any ideas? Do you remember the toast?

Well, here is an idea:
You can think about the three T's -
Think, Thank and Toast.

Think about the awesome time
You had together
Memories which last forever.

Thank 'em for being with you and
For making your wishes come true.

I suggest you make a **Toast**
(I don't mean offering crispy bread)
I'm talking about wishing them well
And making it a true farewell!

You're allowed to feel sad and blue
For a millisecond or two!
But then it's time
To end this rhyme
And focus on the coming time!

'Not just bye' is a beautifully illustrated and touching story that acknowledges and validates one of the challenges that children face: It is hard to say good-bye to loved ones and fun times. It is written from a child's perspective and is simple to understand; for example, it explains what a 'toast' is. Young children are just learning life coping skills and I believe that this book recognizes the difficulty of facing good-byes and also offers solutions to dealing with the same. This, in turn, will educate children in problem-solving in other areas of life.

Charis

PRINTING FOR LIFE

Printing for Life is a boutique publishing company which originated in Australia and developed further with editorial members based in Canada, the United States and Germany. Printing for Life was created to publish Stories for Life with children in mind, believing that a narrative can not only be entertaining and educational but also therapeutic at the same time. This concept is termed narrative medicine and has received increasing attention over the last decade. The stories published by Printing for Life are meant to connect the author and the reader, as well as the illustrator and editorial staff and to remind each one of their own life and purpose. That's why the series is called Stories for Life.

Saying goodbye can be challenging for children and adults alike.

How can you make saying 'bye' good?

In this captivating and beautifully illustrated story for children,

a young boy discovers an answer to this challenge.

Based on a real-life event.

ISBN 978-0-9940339-0-1

90000

9 780994 033901